Roots
BEFORE
Fruits

AN INNOVATIVE BIBLE STUDY
FOR THE NEW CHILD OF GOD

ART WILSON

Critical Mass Books
Davenport, Florida

www.criticalmasspublishing.com

Cover Design: Eowyn Riggins
Interior Layout   Rachel Greene

Unless otherwise indicated, scriptures used throughout this book are from the King James Version.

CONTENTS

FOREWORD

Remnants

(2020-THE PARADIGM SHIFT)

Isaiah 54:17 says: *"No weapon that is formed against thee shall prosper; and every tongue that shall rise against thee in judgment thou shalt condemn. This is the heritage of the servants of the Lord, and their righteousness is of me, saith the Lord."*[1]

In 2020, our world was greatly shaken by a global pandemic. This is the first time our generation has seen anything quite like it. It was not just a physical shaking, but something has also changed in the Spirit. Because of the pandemic, restrictions remain in our world, and things are not as easy as they once were. Even when we gather, things can seem a little stiff because there is a culture of restraint all around us. Fear has risen and anxiety has been prevalent. For us to overcome, we have to purposefully put more effort into tearing down strongholds and investing more time in our walk with God. Some of us have had it too easy, coasting our way through life. But this shaking can be a good thing to help us grow. It has definitely been a wake-up call, and we need to apply ourselves like never before.

When we have a determined attitude, we are saying nothing is going to stop us from praising our Lord in His house—nothing can stand in our way. It's like Paul said in *Romans 8:38-39: "For I am persuaded, that neither death, nor life, nor angels, nor principalities, nor powers, nor things present, nor things to come, Nor height, nor depth, nor any other creature, shall be able to separate us from the love of God, which is in Christ Jesus our Lord."*

Nothing can separate us.

I believe there is power in praise, and where there is much praise, there is much power. And where there is little praise, there is little power. Praise changes the atmosphere and brings the strong presence of God in our lives.

This book is the result of a burden placed on my heart at the dawning of this decade. We are about to explore information that will be vital to the church of the Living God as we embark into a paradigm shift. At first, I thought the material would become a short sermon series, but we are now bringing these thoughts to print. I believe that what this book has to say can make a real difference for months and years to come.

Art Wilson
April 2023

ONE

Remnants

In Isaiah 37:31 says, *"And the remnant that is escaped of the house of Judah shall again take root downward, and bear fruit upward."* This verse is a detailed revelation that speaks of a remnant escaping from bondage.

There are so many things that have the potential to hinder our walk with God. There are things that can restrain us, making it hard to break free. But we must break free. We have no other option. The prophet said there will be a remnant that knows how to escape. And when this happens, *"the house of Judah shall again take root downward, and bear fruit upward."*

I want you to clearly understand the word "remnant." It means a small number, in effect, a *microcosm*. We are now shifting into a world of remnants. In fact, those in positions of authority in our government seem to emphasize this. They have even tried to limit how many people can congregate together in one place. They are trying to isolate people for a specific time and season.

At first, many of us thought the pandemic was going to be a wake-up call for the church. We are now worried that it may be doing the exact opposite. There seems to be a spirit of "slumber" overshadowing God's people. We are starting to hear excuses and are witnessing the development of fear, or a lack of urgency to be physically in the house of God. People still go to work, go shopping, and accomplish all of their day to day needs. However, for some people, that focus and urgency has not been directed towards Godly things. That lets you know that this is a spiritual battle and the devil is very much at work.

There is an extremely important prophetic word that we must examine:

> *"Work at living in peace with everyone, and work at living a holy life, for those who are not holy will not see the Lord. Look after each other so that none of you fails to receive the grace of God. Watch out that no poisonous root of bitterness grows up to trouble you, corrupting many. Make sure that no one is immoral or*

godless like Esau, who traded his birthright as the firstborn son for a single meal. You know that afterward, when he wanted his father's blessing, he was rejected. It was too late for repentance, even though he begged with bitter tears. You have not come to a physical mountain, to a place of flaming fire, darkness, gloom, and whirlwind, as the Israelites did at Mount Sinai. For they heard an awesome trumpet blast and a voice so terrible that they begged God to stop speaking. They staggered back under God's command: "If even an animal touches the mountain, it must be stoned to death." Moses himself was so frightened at the sight that he said, 'I am terrified and trembling. No, you have come to Mount Zion, to the city of the living God, the heavenly Jerusalem, and to countless thousands of angels in a joyful gathering. You have come to the assembly of God's firstborn children, whose names are written in heaven. You have come to God himself, who is the judge over all things. You have come to the spirits of the righteous ones in heaven who have now been made perfect. You have come to Jesus, the one who mediates the new covenant between God *and people, and to the sprinkled blood, which speaks of forgiveness instead of crying out for vengeance like the blood of Abel.' Be careful that you do not refuse to listen to the One who is speaking. For if the people of Israel did not escape when they refused to listen to Moses, the earthly messenger, we will certainly not escape if we reject the One who speaks to us from heaven. When God spoke from Mount Sinai his voice shook the earth, but now he makes another promise: 'Once again I will shake not only the earth but the heavens also.' This means that all of creation will be shaken and removed, so that only unshakable things will remain. Since we are receiving a Kingdom that is unshakable, let us be thankful and please God by worshiping him with holy fear and awe. For our God is a devouring fire."*

—HEBREWS 12:14-29 NLT

THIS PARADIGM HAS SHIFTED

What makes a strong Christian? What makes a person grow weaker through adversity and yet, another person grow stronger? Let's begin our discussion about *Roots before Fruits*. We all know that it is impossible to have *fruit* without *roots*, however we seldom think about roots. The fruit is what we want. Even though we cannot see the roots under the surface hidden from plain sight, it does not lessen the fact that the fruit is only possible when the roots are *healthy*.

What we witness happening before our eyes in the natural world can actually apply as a principal example of what can be happening in the spirit world. The Bible often uses natural laws and physical examples to describe the unseen spiritual world that is all around us. We too often desire the benefits and taste of the fruit, but we can ignore the essential condition of our roots. We can often neglect what is important in our pursuits to possess what we want. Let us be aware of what will keep us strong—our roots.

God has given His church some powerful resources. We are reminded in Mark 16:16-18 KJV, *"He that believeth and is baptized shall be saved;*

but he that believeth not shall be damned. And these signs shall follow them that believe; In my name shall they cast out devils; they shall speak with new tongues; They shall take up serpents; and if they drink any deadly thing, it shall not hurt them; they shall lay hands on the sick, and they shall recover."

We love this scripture, and we shout and preach about it. We love to talk about this kind of power, for it belongs to God. Jesus gave power to His church, and if you are a believer, you are entitled to this power. We celebrate the nine gifts of the Spirit, and we anticipate the moving of God. Let us remember the Bible tells us to covet and pursue them because they edify the church. They build us up and empower us.

I recently asked my children, "Do you remember when we used to travel on the mission field and evangelistic field?" (This was when they were very young.) I asked, "Do you remember the great things we saw and the miracles that took place?" We saw devils cast out of people. We saw the power of God move throughout the Body of

Christ all over the world. It was truly amazing to witness.

But now things have changed a bit. We are now living in a different day—a time of remnants. We will see even greater acts of God in our future. However, our methods may change, our approach may evolve, but the future is going to demand a greater and more passionate walk with God for all of us if we are going to successfully be a part of this paradigm shift.

We must re-establish our roots.

_____

Isaiah 37:31

Hebrews 12:14-29 NLT

Mark 16:17-18

TWO

Palm Trees

Many people in the church today are content with the status quo. They are content with being spiritually lukewarm and have little or no desire to pursue spiritual victory or breakthrough. They lack the kind of conviction they once had. It's gone.

We used to have services where we didn't go home until we received a real breakthrough. We refused to say "Amen" until everyone was delivered. We'd keep singing until there was a breakthrough. There was a term for it—*tarrying*. Tarrying meant that no one left the service until they received what they needed from God.

Now it seems that we are seeing remnants of those past revivals, and we often leave our services with strongholds yet to be broken. The heritage of the church of the living God is historic. We would come to the house of God and sit under powerful preaching. Just listening to the Word of God gripped our hearts so intensely that we would grab the pew bracing ourselves under the conviction we felt.

The Lord spoke through his mighty prophet, Isaiah, *"You will dig your roots downward and you will bear fruit upwards."* The sad fact is that we all-too-often find ourselves becoming content living without roots.

I want to share with you a story about my wife, Bethany, and the landscaping outside of our home. When you look at the plants they look beautiful, but if you look more closely, they can deceive you. They look almost perfect, but then you reach out and touch them and to your surprise, they are plastic. Not all of them are artificial, but some are.

I looked outside at her plants one day, and I saw a bee buzzing around them. Suddenly, the bee dove right into one of the fake flowers. Have you ever seen a confused bee? I'm sure the bee was thinking, "Somebody help me. What's going on here? Is this the Apocalypse?" He had confused an artificial plant for a real one. The real flowers and plants were surrounded by insects, but the plastic ones were eventually left alone.

You see, an artificial plant can impersonate one that has real fruit, but it will never have *roots*. You can't fake roots, but you can impersonate fruit. God is calling us back to Him and to the reality and the understanding that we must work on roots before we can have authentic fruit.

Did you know people who have strong healthy roots will raise their hands and praise the Lord in the midst of any situation, no matter how difficult? Their roots make this possible. In the very first Psalm it says, *"And he shall be like a tree planted by the rivers, that bringeth forth his fruit in his season; his leaf also shall not wither; and whatsoever he doeth shall prosper."[1]*

This is why God is calling the church to dig deeper. We must do this before we can truly move upward. We should never talk about fruit until we first discuss in detail the health of our roots. I want us to explore how we can thrive and have great revival in our personal lives and as a result, explosive growth in the church of living God in this

[1] *Psalm 1:3 (KJV)*

hour. I have embarked on a study that compares the symbolic similarities of the health of the tree and the health of the people of God.

BENEATH THE SOIL

Our problems are not on the surface. They are not superficial. People don't fall away or *backslide* overnight. It always starts with something that happens *below the surface*. In fact, there is always something going on out of sight. Problems start with something deeply sinister inside. This may be hard to face, and as you read on things may get a little uncomfortable, but that is what it takes to develop Godly roots.

The battle may not be obvious to you, but after a while the fight going on below the surface will start to break through and you'll see evidence on the surface. People seldom quit serving the Lord at a moment's notice. There has always been "under the surface" erosion in such cases. This is why we need to protect our roots.

Of course, we need to understand that the devil knows if he can get to our roots, he never has to worry about our fruits. We read in 1 Peter 5: 8, *"Be sober, be vigilant; because your adversary the devil, as a roaring lion, walketh about, seeking whom he may devour."* He wants to be able to just walk by and destroy you. He is a master of observing lukewarm Christians and knows the weaker you are, the harder it is for you to have strong roots. God is calling us to dig downward before we talk about anything happening upward.

Trees are a great example of strong roots. It has been determined that the depth of a particular tree's roots is a true indicator of its strength and power to stand no matter what. Show me the roots, and I'll tell you how powerful that tree is. It doesn't really matter how tall it is, it matters how *deep* it is.

When you encounter a child of God who doesn't seem to be interested in the things of the Lord, we might think that it is a matter of someone not bearing fruit. As a Christian, we know that fruit is important and vital to our walk with God.

In Galatians 5:22-23 it says, *"But the fruit of the Spirit is love, joy, peace, longsuffering, gentleness, goodness, faith, meekness, temperance: against such there is no law."* As we grow in Christ, these characteristics begin to take root, and so does our desire to work for the Kingdom. John 15:8 reads, *"Herein is my Father glorified, that ye bear much fruit; so shall ye be my disciples."* Always remember the evidence of being a disciple is to have fruit.

If you have the power of the Holy Ghost, sooner or later you're going to have to do something for God. If you're not currently being used by God to work in His Kingdom and you do not have a sense of urgency to get involved, it is an indicator that there is something wrong under the surface. How can you be content not achieving when you have such a valuable treasure in your earthen vessel? I pray that the Holy Ghost speaks to you as you grow deeper roots and show you how you can be an influence for Him. We believe that God will open even greater doors, by giving you the grace to do something great.

The first tree we need to examine is the *palm* tree. This represents the Christian who knows how to "*bend.*" They say the palm tree is one of the most unique trees you'll ever find. A palm tree is able to bend 50 degrees in a storm without snapping or breaking. It's a tree that has figured out what the Bible means when it says in Romans 8:35-39, " *Who shall separate us from the love of Christ? Shall tribulation, or distress, or persecution, or famine, or nakedness, or peril, or sword? As it is written, for thy sake we are killed all the day long; we are accounted as sheep for the slaughter. Nay, in all these things we are more than conquerors through Him that loved us. For I am persuaded, that neither death, nor life, nor angels, nor principalities, nor powers, nor things present, nor things to come, Nor height, nor depth, nor any other creature, shall be able to separate us from the love of God, which is in Christ Jesus our Lord.*" So many children of God need a *palm tree spirit*. They need to learn to bend without breaking. Then, the next time someone asks, "How are you doing?" You can simply reply, "I'm bending with the breeze even if it's a hurricane wind."

With roots, we can have much more bend than break. In other words, we have *righteous flexibility*. When the strongest winds blow and the most brutal storms are raging around you, that palm tree will survive. The palm tree's secret is that it has deep roots. Deep roots are exactly what we are going to need if we are to make it when the world around us seems to be falling apart.

We have to learn and teach these principles in our local churches.

In this hour, we cannot let the raging storms snap us in half. We must be strong in facing the pressures of this world with its social media and other pressures. Let nothing "snap" you—you're going to have to learn how to bend.

God will always help us. In the book of Psalms 46:1 it says, *"God is our refuge and strength, a very present help in trouble."* In a sense, He wants us to learn that there is more to us than meets the eye.

The next time you look in the mirror, you need to tell yourself: "There is more to me than this."

In Luke 22:31-33, Jesus said essentially this same thing to Simon Peter: *"And the Lord said, Simon, Simon, behold, Satan hath desired to have you, that he may sift you as wheat: But I have prayed for thee, that thy faith fail not: and when thou art converted, strengthen thy brethren."* So if you don't think God truly loves you, you have forgotten about the cross and the sacrifice that was given. If the Lord loved us enough to die for us, surely, He loves us enough to take care of us.

When you make mistakes and you feel like you're failing, God is making intercession for you. There is nothing that will separate you from His love.

In Psalms 56:12, it says, *"Thy vows are upon me, O God: I will render praises unto thee."* The Lord said to Peter in Luke 22:32-34, *"But I have prayed for thee, that thy faith fail not: and when thou art converted, strengthen thy brethren. And he said unto him, Lord, I am ready to go with thee, both into prison, and to death. And he said, I tell thee, Peter, the cock shall not crow this day, before that thou shalt thrice deny that thou knowest me.*"

In other words, Jesus was telling Peter, "A storm is about to happen in your life but the storm will not hurt you. In fact, it's going to *convert* you and change you incredibly. "And after the storm fixes you, you are to go forth and fix someone else." Think of it like this, "Hey Peter, the enemy is coming. You're going to lose, but don't break. I'm praying for you while you're failing." Peter was like a palm tree because he didn't break during persecution. We all need to hear this message. We all need this mindset. Let the storm happen, because through the storm, we learn how to let adversity make us stronger. We are digging deeper again to have strong roots.

Speaking of strong roots, palm trees can lay all the way down in a storm, and then when the storm is over, they bounce right back up. Isn't that amazing? God can do that through you. You can continue to be effective no matter the severity of your storm.

According to *www.hunker.com/palmtree* research, there are many factors contributing to a palm's ability to withstand wind, including the tree's age, whether it is native or exotic, the condition of the soil, the duration of the storm, and whether the tree grows on its own or among other trees. The Huffington Post suggests, with a strong trunk and open canopy, palms are wind-resistant. Plus, palms fold into themselves when they catch a gust of wind. In some cases, that helps the tree hold onto its foliage through a storm.

Can you see why roots are so important? They get us through the storm and on our way to fruit. We are going to explore some things that will make us stronger and wiser. As you read these words, I want you to lift up your hands and begin to receive strength, power, and receive anointing in the name of Jesus, we shall have roots. Regardless of what has knocked us down, we are overcomers.

We need to dig and dig down deep.

REMNANT MINDSET

Now, according to the prophetic word in Isaiah 37:31-32—*"And the remnant that is escaped of the house of Judah shall again take root downward, and bear fruit upward; For out of Jerusalem shall go forth a remnant and they that escape out of Mount Zion: the zeal of the Lord of hosts shall do this."*— there will always be a group of people called a remnant who will escape the grip of decline. They will buck against the trend. They will swim against the tide. These people will be all about praise. They will faithfully dig downward during the storm. They will stand firm when the storm comes at them in its full fury.

Such people are like the Apostle Paul when he was in prison at Philippi. He was in custody through no fault of his own and simply trying to do God's will. But when you actively try to turn the world upside down, you can stir up a storm of controversy and conflict. How did Paul and his co-laborers handle things when they were in a dark and primitive prison?

"And at midnight Paul and Silas prayed, and sang praises unto God: and the prisoners heard them. And suddenly there was a great earthquake, so that the foundations of the prison were shaken: and immediately all the doors were opened, and everyone's bands were loosed. And the innkeeper of the prison awaking out of his sleep, and seeing the prison doors open, he drew out his sword, and would have killed himself, supposing that the prisoners had been fled. But Paul cried with a loud voice, saying, 'Do thyself no harm: for we are all here.' Then he called for a light, and sprang in, and came trembling, and fell down before Paul and Silas. And brought them out, and said, 'Sirs, what must I do to be saved?' And they said, 'believe on the Lord Jesus Christ and thou shalt be saved, and thy house.' And they spake unto him the word of the Lord, and to all that were in his house. And he took them the same hour of the night, and washed their stripes; and was baptized, and he all his, straightway. And when he had brought them into his house, he set meat before them, and rejoiced, believing in God with all his house."

—ACTS 16:25-34 (KJV)

They sang praises because they had roots, and as a result of having roots, it produced fruits. The jailor and his household were gloriously saved. You can tell a lot about your roots and how deep they are by how you handle adversity. If you have a true heart of praise, your roots are good. If you complain and find yourself spiraling down to despair, check your roots. There could be an issue below the surface.

Let's revisit that idea of "remnants" and Isaiah 37:31—*"And the remnant that is escaped of the house of Judah shall again take root downward, and bear fruit upward."* It is vital that we understand the sequence. In this current hour of the church, we are entering a paradigm shift. We are approaching a time of remnants. Just as in Noah's day when there were just eight who entered into the ark of God and were spared the tragedy of that day. Noah did not surrender to defeat brought on by superficial spirituality.

We must be like Shadrach, Meshach, and Abednego, who refused to give in to peer pressure, and who stood in the face of adversity and refused to bow to the idols standing before them. We must be prepared as a small remnant to oppose the antichrists of the whole world, if necessary. Just like in the book of Acts in the upper room, the disciples took the power of the Holy Ghost into the streets and turned their world upside down. God does not hesitate to work through remnants. The Lord will work through even a small number of committed people and history teaches us that with God all things are possible.

When the COVID pandemic first began, we thought it would be a mighty wake-up call for God's people. As time moved on, we had to face the sad fact that the opposite was indeed happening for some. It seemed that people took advantage of the liberty that came from our collective "time out," and many started growing cold. But during that time, the Lord spoke to me and said "You need to give the church and the world a message about *trees*." We need to study their attributes and learn from their stability. Let us strive to be what it says in Psalm 1:3, *"And he shall be like a tree…"*.

Be a palm tree for the Lord.

Psalms 1:3 KJV

1 Peter 5:8 KJV

Galatians 5:22-23 KJV

John 15:8 KJV

Romans 8:35-39 KJV

Psalms 46:1 KJV

Luke 22:31-32 KJV

Psalms 56:12 KJV

Luke 22:32-34 KJV

Isaiah 37:31-32 KJV

Acts 16:25-34 KJV

THREE

Fight for Your Faith.

We talk a lot about the great and powerful resources we receive from God. We even boast, shout, and dance about them (and we should). We get excited about blessings and what God is doing in our lives. We believe with all of our hearts what is said in Mark 16:16-18: "*He that believeth and is baptized shall be saved; but he that believeth not shall be damned. And these signs shall follow them that believe; in my name they shall cast out devils; they shall speak with new tongues; They shall take up serpents; and if they drink any deadly thing, it shall not hurt them; they shall lay hands on the sick, and they shall recover.*"

We get excited about the gifts of the Spirit. We shout about walking on water and raising the dead. But we need to realize that these things only happen when our roots have intentionally been planted and strengthened.

"You shall be like a tree…".

When we study the principle of deep and unshakable roots, the perfect analogy—as we have already seen—is the palm tree. We need to be flexible and able to bend, but not break. So many are breaking today because they don't have deep enough roots. We can learn so much from what God teaches us through nature and we need to see what He's showing us about roots.

THE STRENGTH OF YOUR ROOTS

The strength of your roots is of utmost importance because it will determine how much pressure or stress you can handle. Without strong enough (meaning deep enough) roots, the storm can come and break you, or worse, it can rip you right out of the ground. The key is faith, which comes and grows by hearing the Word of God. You must have faith. And you often have to fight for that faith.

There is a constant struggle in America with mediocrity and our approach to the miraculous. If we are not careful, we can even become casual. We can become so used to the supernatural that great reports have no effect on us. This is why we need to have an ongoing discussion about faith. Unless we begin with faith, we can't go any further. Without faith, you're not going to have any real stability in your life. But if you believe, you have strength. And if you believe, you shall not perish. John 3:16 says, *"For God so loved the world, that he gave his only begotten Son, that <u>whosoever believeth</u>…"*.

Do you know that the opposite of doing evil is *not* doing good? It's because doing good is based on your own judgment. The Bible never says the opposite of doing evil is doing good. But according to John 3:20-21, it says, *"For every one that doeth evil hateth the light, neither cometh to the light, lest his deeds should be reproved. But he that doeth truth cometh to the light, that his deeds may be made manifest, that they are wrought in God."*

The verse says, "But he that doeth truth." The truth is the opposite of evil because truth comes from God and disobedience to the truth is evil. Believing leads to truth. Unbelief leads to evil. You have to have truth if you want to do good. In other words, God tells you what is truth and God's truth is good. Truth is not an opinion, it's a fact.

In other words, God is telling us that whether we believe in the Kingdom of God or not, it's still true. It doesn't matter if you believe in Heaven or not, it's still true. Not believing doesn't make it untrue. Whether you believe in Hell or not, it is still real. If you're going to have strong roots, you're going to have to believe in the truth. Scripture gives us proof of the power of belief.

" Jesus said unto him, if thou canst believe, all things are possible to him that believeth."

—MARK 9:23

"But without faith it is impossible to please him: for he that cometh to God must believe that he is, and that he is a rewarder of them that diligently seek him."

—HEBREWS 11:6

"And these signs shall follow them that believe; in my name shall they cast out devils; they shall speak with new tongues."

—MARK 16:17

Do not let the devil take your faith. Fight for it. Contend for it. Take up its shield. You have to work on your faith if you want to have strong roots. When trials come your way, you won't be uprooted. With strong roots, doubt will have no place and you can boldly say, "I'm going to believe the Lord's report."

THE DEPTHS OF YOUR ROOTS

A really good tree knows how to dig deep. I'm told when trees find a good place they wrap their roots around everything they can (rocks, boulders, pipes, etc.). The tree will just keep on digging. Some children of God are in trouble because they have stopped digging. When you dig, it creates depth, which takes you deeper into prayer. Prayer leads you deeper into a relationship with God which leads to worship. Worship leads to shouting, then to dancing, and then to running—and it all starts with digging.

Deep folks know how to praise God and dig down, even in the tough times, and still praise Him. I'm told that trees try to go as deep downward as they are tall upward. How can we expect to grow upward without digging deeper spiritually? You have to learn how to pray. Prayer is of the utmost importance. We have to learn how to talk to God, to pray when we feel like it and when we don't. Sometimes you will find yourself in difficult situations, keep on digging. Don't stop until you breakthrough. Pray in tongues, for we know not to pray as we should, but the Spirit begins to pray through us (more on this specific discussion later). When the Spirit takes over, He starts to talk and pray in all kinds of fluent languages. He starts to go to war for you. You might not even know what you're supposed to pray about, but the Spirit knows. All because you're digging deeper roots.

The Bible says when you pray in tongues you build *yourself* up. Speaking in tongues is not just one of the nine Gifts of the Spirit. Those who do not know the Word think that tongues are not essential in their walk with God. Don't miss out on the blessing and power we have access to through the Spirit. When you speak in tongues, you're born of the Spirit, and once you're born of the Spirit, there are seeds of power you can potentially possess, but not until you are born of the Spirit. When you are born of the Spirit, you will speak in tongues. The same way a baby cries out when he's born into this world, you cry out when you're born of the Holy Ghost.

For example, the Bible tells us in 1 Corinthians 14:2, *"For he that speaketh in an unknown tongue speaketh not unto men, but unto God: for no man understandeth him; howbeit in the spirit he speaketh mysteries."* In this passage, we get clarity about the baptism of the Holy Ghost. You are not speaking to man, this is not the gift of tongues to be spoken to man or the congregation. This is the baptism of the Holy Ghost and when you pray in the Spirit, you are speaking directly to God. But when you're operating in the gift of tongues, that is for man. This passage of scripture says further, *"…howbeit in the spirit he speaketh mysteries. He that speaketh in an unknown tongue edifieth himself; but he that prophesieth…"* The Holy Ghost is able to both bless you and then bless somebody else. They call it *prophesying*. This is further explained in 1 Corinthians 14:3: *"But he that prophesieth speaketh unto men to edification, and exhortation, and comfort."*

You have to learn how to pray to tap into this power.

Then he says, *"He that speaketh in an unknown tongue edifieth himself; but he that prophesieth edifieth the church."* You speak in tongues to go where you have never been. This is the key to deeper roots. When you pray, you go where *you* know. When you speak in tongues, God takes you where you don't know.

The Bible calls it a *mystery*.

Mark 16:16-18 KJV

John 3:16 KJV

John 3:20-21 KJV

Mark 9:23

Hebrews 11:6

Mark 16:17

1 Corinthians 14:2-3

FOUR

Roots Must Be Watered

The next thing we need to learn about roots is that they have to be *watered*. How do you water? Sometimes a tree finds water and it literally latches on to the source, as in: *"You shall be like a tree planted by water…"*

Water is very simple. Scripture tells us it is the Word. Ephesians 5:26 says, *"That he might sanctify and cleanse it with the washing of water by the word,"* Without the Word, you're going to dry up. Without the Word, you're going to wither away. Without the Word, you're not going to make it. Without the Word, you're going to be brittle and prone to snapping, you're going to lack the help you need. We need the Word of God.

David said in Psalms 119:11, *"Thy word have I hid in my heart, that I might not sin against thee."* You not only need to believe the Word of God, but you need to have a thirst and desire for the Word. When you do, you will have refreshing, energizing, and cleansing water for your roots.

The longest chapter in the Bible is Psalms 119. Do you know why Psalms 119 is one of the most unique chapters in all the Bible? When it was written, it had eight divisions, and in those eight divisions, the writer was able to highlight each division with a letter from the Hebrew alphabet. The first division is *Aleph*. The second division is *Bet* in Hebrew. Do you know why they call it *Bet* or *Beth*? *The root meaning of Bet is* house. When the Psalmist began to write the second division of *Bet*, he chose to feature his discussion about the Word, because in every house, the feature should be the Word. Looking at the New Living Translation, the second division, starts in Psalms 119:9 and runs through verse 16. It says, *"How can a young person stay pure? By obeying your word. I have tried hard to find you—don't let me wander from your commands. I have hidden your word in my heart, that I might not sin against you. I praise you, O Lord; teach me your decrees, I have recited aloud all the regulations you have given us. I have rejoiced in your laws as much as in riches. I will study your commandments and reflect on your ways. I will delight in your decrees and not forget your word."*

You need the Word.

I can appreciate a person who loves to study many resources and gain knowledge from many books and commentaries that are based on the Word of God. However, all of these resources people are reading can never replace it. Don't give something else authority over the Word of God. *"Thy word have I hid in mine heart, that I might not sin against thee."* It is of the utmost importance that the people of God understand that without His Word, there will be no water and you'll wither up and eventually die.

THE STABILITY OF THE ROOTS

A tree puts a premium on stability. The tree instinctively works to safeguard itself from all potential danger. Scientists are now discovering that plants react to things. Plants don't want to be uprooted. Trees know how to link up together through their rooting system. This principle is a perfect illustration that the church of the living

God can benefit from. We are simply stronger when we support one another and protect one another. In this hour, we need to create a culture of unity and resist division at all costs. Do you know how to link up? If somebody is in trouble and you link up, then they've got your back and you've got theirs. We can't do this alone—we need the local church.

They tell me that one of the most dangerous things you could do to any kind of plant, is to uproot it and replant it in a different location. They say transferring any vegetation to other areas greatly increases the percentage of its death. For a tree to successfully re-establish itself in foreign soil, it must be planted in the right condition and that will nurture healthy and sustainable growth. If trees could talk, I believe the tree would say, "Please don't move me."

The Lord said, "You shall be like a tree planted..." meaning, when God plants you, He does not want you to move. I want you here and where I put you, I want you to stay. In 1

Corinthians 15:58, Paul says, *"Therefore, my beloved brethren, be ye steadfast, unmovable, always abounding in the work of the Lord, for as much as ye know that your labour is not in vain in the Lord."* There is a very interesting label that talks about an issue trees can experience when they are not relocated correctly. They have all kinds of terms for it, but I like this one the best. They call it, *Tree Transplant Shock.*

A tree can actually go into shock when it's moved incorrectly.

Symptoms of Tree Transplant Shock incl wilting, scorching, browning leaves, or early onset of fall colors. Trees that grow with a compromised root system will have limited water availability and may send the wrong signals to foliage, creating off-season coloration or in the worst-case scenarios, death.

They tell me that after Hurricane Katrina when they scanned the areas, they found something unusual. One breed of tree was unmoved. It wasn't the palm tree, because there are few palms in New Orleans, it was another kind of tree. This one had a different methodology. It's the *Giant Oak,* but its strength is not bending and comes from sticking together in clusters. These trees have devised a system where they grow close together and intertwine their rooting system, making them virtually immovable, as long as they stick together.

THE TREE AND THE SEED

Let's talk about the tree and the seed. It is the ultimate cause and effect. When Jesus was talking to his disciples about the vine and the branches in John 15:8, he declared, *"When you produce much fruit, you are my true disciples. This brings great glory to my Father."* The scripture is clear that without a doubt, God wants his people to be fruit-bearers. Now, what does this mean? In the Book of Galatians 5:22-23, we see, *"But the fruit of the Spirit is love, joy, peace, long-suffering, gentleness, goodness, faith, meekness, temperance: against such there is no law."* In other words, when the Holy Ghost is the dominant force in our lives, certain positive character and emotional traits will be evident and obvious.

There is, however, another kind of fruit that God is interested in seeing develop in us—*reproduction*. We need to win souls for Christ. In Proverbs 11:30 it says, *"The fruit of the righteous is a tree of life and he that winneth souls is wise."* The fruit of the righteous is a *tree*. The symbolism is unmistakable. Of course, before any fruit can be produced we need the *seed*.

Sadly, we live in a day of "seedless" fruits. We buy fruits that have been modified where some chemical genome has been introduced to remove the seeds. We all know about seedless watermelon, seedless grapes, and so on. Now, this may be better for the person consuming the fruit and not having to deal with the hassle of avoiding seeds while you are eating but when the seeds are removed, the real purpose of the fruit to reproduce and replenish is taken away.

Something to think about.

Have you ever considered that when you walk outside and knock on a tree, it's just a big stick? Yet, from these big sticks, we receive so many different kinds of fruit. How does this happen? Where does a tree get its material to make a banana? We love bananas. We love apples. But they all come from big sticks. It's really amazing.

Have you ever eaten an orange? How about a grapefruit? I had a pomegranate recently and I opened it up and said, "My Lord, only God could make something like this." The "stick" basically uses three things to make all of the delicious fruits we enjoy: soil, water, and sunshine. When the fruit is ripe and ready, it can nourish, refresh, and even heal your body. A banana, for example, can provide the potassium and other nutrients you need to live and grow. How? God.

In the same way, the Lord can take sinful vessels like us and through His miraculous process equip us to bear fruit for the world. Just like an ordinary old stick. Can you imagine?

In 1646, the Westminster Assembly created a reformed statement of faith called the Westminster Confession, part of which goes like this: *"What is the chief and highest end of man? Answer: Man's chief and highest end is to glorify God, and fully to enjoy him forever."* But how do we glorify God? By producing *fruit*. In the book of John 15:16, it says, *"Ye have not chosen me, but I have chosen you, and ordained you, that ye should go and bring forth fruit, and that your fruit should remain: that whatsoever ye shall ask of the Father in my name, He may give it you."* God is going to get the glory out of your life and we shall bring forth fruit.

But we know the answer to our success, and it's nothing but the blood of Jesus. You're going to make it. You're going to bring forth fruit. No one is perfect, and we have all made mistakes but you're going to bear fruit. The victory we all enjoy is because of God's amazing grace. He focuses on repairing us, not destroying us. I have chosen the word repair on purpose. The Lord takes what's broken and fixes it. In the same miraculous way that God can plant a stick in the ground and with His resources produce a variety of beautiful fruit. God is going to prosper you as you get rooted in His spiritual resources.

Why would a tree or a plant go through all of this trouble to make fruit? What is the purpose? The seed. A tree went through all of this to bear fruit in order to spread the seed. Do you know what God wants you to do? He said, *"I would that you bear fruit."* Why? Because in that fruit is a seed. Do you know what a seed does? It reproduces itself after its own kind. God wants us to reproduce other children of God.

The purpose is to spread the seed. When you pray, you spread the seed. When you win a soul, you spread the seed. Do you know why we go through all this trouble to make fruit? We need to make disciples for the Lord. The success of the seed is the purpose for everything.

All plant life benefits from the same resources: sun, water, and soil. Doesn't the Bible mention something quite similar in 1 John 5:8: *"And there are three that bear witness in the earth, the Spirit, and the water, and the blood: and these three agree in one."* God teaches us through nature to let us know what we are intended to do. We're not intended to backslide. We're not intended to live like the devil. We are the people of God. We're supposed to bear fruit, and we're supposed to spread the seed.

The Bible tells us in Psalms 1:3, *"And he shall be like a **tree planted** by the rivers of water, that bringeth forth his fruit in his season; his leaf also shall not wither; and whatsoever he doeth shall prosper."* Whatever adjustments we need to make in our lives, we must do in order to bear fruit. It is important to remember that the first impression that will have an impact on the people you meet, will be your fruit. When you first encounter people, they will seldom discern the depths of your roots, but fruits are always visible to all. In Matthew 7:20 KJV, Jesus emphatically stated, *"Wherefore by their fruits ye shall know them."*

That's why we practice outward holiness. The Bible says in 1 Samuel 16:7, *"But the LORD said unto Samuel, Look not on his countenance, or on the height of his stature; because I have refused him: for the LORD seeth not as man seeth; for man looketh on the outward appearance, but the LORD looketh on the heart."*

Your outward appearance is the greatest witness to people you first meet. People see your outward appearance and they need your witness. If you don't resemble the Kingdom of God, it could be a hindrance when you are trying to impact people for Christ. Let your conversation, which is everything about you, bring glory to God.

What ministry is God calling you to do? How are you supposed to bless the Kingdom of God? Bring forth fruit. The Lord is depending on us to be good fruit.

If you need to repent of something, repent of it right now. If you've lost your way, get back on track right now. We need fruit-bearers. If you've been letting something get in the way of your walk with God, move it out of the way. If God has blessed you with gifts, a voice to sing, a right mind, and a passion to serve Him, He blessed you so that you may bring Him glory and bring fruit to the kingdom.

Ephesians 5:26 KJV

Psalms 119:11 KJV

Psalms 119:9

1 Corinthians 15:58

John 15:8 NLT

Galatians 5:22-23 KJV

Proverbs 11:30 KJV

John 15:16 KJV

1 John 5:8 KJV

Psalms 1:3 KJV

Matthew 7:20 KJV

1 Samuel 16:7 KJV

FIVE

Stand, Therefore

While talking to the Lord, He dropped this word into my spirit, He said, "There are great hidden spiritual truths found in nature all around us. I want you to teach a whole series on some of these things." I began working on messages for our local church (both in-person and online), and with the support of others, we put it in book form.

One of the oldest living things on earth is a tree. They can outlive anything, and in every element and situation, they've learned to survive. I am reminded of "The Survivor Tree" from 9/11. A month after the tragic attacks on the World Trade Center, they found a tree that had survived it all. It was among the ruins. It had broken limbs, a blackened burned trunk, and damaged roots. Yet it stands at the memorial today, fully healthy, as a symbol of strength and resilience. The Lord has said, *You shall be like a tree planted by the waters, and you will bring forth fruit in due time.*

We can get caught up in fruits, but it's hard to have fruits without roots. Earlier in this book, we examined the bend in the palm tree, how it knows how to move and go with the flow with every storm and situation. We also talked about maintaining healthy roots. Now, I want to talk to you about strong and overcoming roots.

I believe if we really grasp these truths, we'll never have to worry about backsliding. With that being said, we read in Romans 1:16, *"For I am not ashamed of the gospel of Christ: for it is the power of God unto salvation to everyone that believeth to the Jew first, and also to the Greek."*

There is a common quality in everyone who overcomes—strong roots. You have to have strong roots if you're going to make it. I'm going to emphasize this by giving you illustrations of people in the Bible who have developed strong roots in unbelievable situations, and God wants you to do the same. If you're going to endure in this hour, you need to realize you have to have strong roots in the Kingdom of God.

The Kingdom of God talks about power in the gospels. The first thing you understand when you get saved, is that you have been born into the power of God. God didn't mean for you to have a one-time dose of power. He wants you to have waves of power. God meant for you to have power whenever you need it.

When a situation or circumstance comes your way, God wants you to have all the power you need. Jesus said in Luke 10:19, *"Behold I give unto you power to tread on serpents and scorpions, and over all the power of the enemy: and nothing shall by any means hurt you."* God gave you enough power to win, and what you can't beat, He gave you the power to outlast. In James 4:7, it says, *"Submit yourselves therefore to God. Resist the devil, and he will flee from you."* What you can't outlast, God gave you power to overcome. Revelation 21:7 says, *"He that overcometh shall inherit all things; and I will be his God, and he shall be my son."* He gave you power for every situation and circumstance. Why? Because God wants you to have victory in every situation.

If you're going to make it, you're going to have to develop and nurture the roots God has given you, and you need His power to do so. God wants you to be able to stand. *"Having done all, to stand. Stand, therefore."* He talks a lot about enduring and standing. Why? Jesus didn't raise any wimps. God is telling you that you have to learn how to be strong.

We love the incredible miraculous story of Lazarus. Lazarus had been dead for four days and Jesus was very particular about what He directed them to do in order for Lazarus to receive his miracle. He said, "*You* roll the stone away. *I'll* raise him from the dead."

Jesus is an all-powerful and all-knowing God. He could snap His fingers and roll the stone away. Isn't there a time in the Bible that He miraculously had the stone rolled away? Yes, when it was time for the Lord God Almighty to come out of the tomb that was holding Him. A mighty angel rolled the stone away. But this time the Lord wants us to roll the stone away? Why does He want us to roll the stone away this time and He had the stone rolled away when He was in the tomb? The answer is very simple. God knows you're capable of handling it, so He will not baby you, because He expects you to be strong. He *will* do what you *cannot* do, but He will *not* do what you *can* do.

Back in the days of the Billy Graham crusades on television, there was this mighty singer who regularly sang the wonderful song, *His Eye is on the Sparrow.* Her name was Ethel Waters. She was such a vibrant woman of faith and liked to say, "God don't sponsor no flops."

The Bible is a military book. It talks about warfare. It talks about the armor of God. It talks about power. It talks about weaponry. It talks about engaging in battle, spiritually and physically. This Bible is not some book about a cruise ship where you just sit back and people wait on you hand and foot. You are not living in utopia every day since you spoke in tongues. This ship we are riding into glory is more like a battleship. God shows up with a sword and a shield and gives that to *you*. It says in Ephesians 6:13, " *Wherefore take unto you the* armor of God, that ye may be able to withstand in the evil day, and having done all, to stand."

We are His ambassadors. When He gave us the Holy Ghost, He gave us more of Him so that we can be overcomers, and we have to have strong roots in this life. We understand that some battles He will fight for you, when He knows you can't fight it alone. The Bible says in 1 Corinthians 10:13, *"There hath no temptation taken you but such as is common to man: but God is faithful, who will not suffer you to be tempted above that ye are able; but will with the temptation also make a way to escape, that ye may be able to bear it."* God will provide even a way of escape when necessary. But in the times He doesn't, He's looking for *you* to be strong in the Lord.

Romans 1:16 KJV

Luke 10:19 KJV

James 4:7 KJV

Revelation 21:7 KJV

Ephesians 6:13 KJV
1 Corinthians 10:13 KJV

SIX

An Enemy is There

The older I get, the more I realize and understand that the toughest people on earth are Christians. Anybody can quit this. Anybody can walk away from this. But it takes a powerful person to *stay* in this. The toughest people on the planet are the people who stay in church.

In times of great trials and tribulations, it may seem easier to walk away. It may seem easier to give in to sin and let the devil step all over you, because you have problems. It's important to have the right perspective. Did you know that everyone has troubles? Even the greatest in the kingdom of God has to endure hard times. Even the most spiritual in the church has to endure hard times. It takes a powerful person to learn how to stand in this evil day. Stand and stay is what the Lord is telling us. Don't give up. And if you fall and come up short, get back up and try again. The Bible tells us emphatically in Proverbs 24:16, *"For a just man falleth seven times, and riseth up again: but the wicked shall fall into mischief."* Keep getting back up. We are told in James 4:7, *"Submit yourselves therefore to*

God. Resist the devil, and he will flee from you." If you keep the mentality that the Apostle James is talking about, and don't give up, eventually the devil will give up and leave you. Keep getting back up.

The Lord wants us to become people who know how to fight the good fight of faith. If we don't defend ourselves spiritually and learn how to identify spiritual warfare, our highly motivated enemy will get an advantage and he will continue to attack us. The enemy comes in to look for areas of weakness.

Be strong.

One of the most deceptive attacks from the enemy is the "familiar spirit". A familiar spirit operates differently than a demon or a beast. Paul said in 1 Corinthians 15:32, *"If after the manner of men I have fought with beasts at Ephesus, what advantageth me, if the dead rise not? Let us eat and drink; for tomorrow we die."* In my ministry, there were times when I had spiritual warfare with beasts. There have been times in powerful prayer meetings where we have seen devils cast out of people. However, spiritual warfare with a familiar spirit is quite different. Sometimes, it can be more complicated removing familiar spirits out of someone's life. The Bible calls them *familiar* spirits. They are familiar. People get to know them. People adopt a familiar spirit's habits. People can even depend on familiar spirits. They have become familiar. If a person has managed to become attached to a familiar spirit, it may be more complicated to get them delivered permanently.

The way a familiar spirit works is through deception. It can often appear as an angel of light. It can impersonate whatever is necessary to gain access into your life. Then it attaches itself to you like a symbiont or a host, and it begins to give you directions that are anti-God. This is why it is extremely important for the saints of God to have a spiritual covering. At times like this when you are confused, you need to speak to your pastor or church leadership and get direction because a familiar spirit specializes in deception. Its purpose is to separate you from the kingdom of God. The familiar spirit is very cunning. It watches you and attacks you in areas that you struggle (giving, worship, sin, holiness, or submission). Make sure that you surround yourself with people that you can be accountable to so that you are never deceived by these attacks.

When dealing with any kind of demon, beast, or aggressive spirit, simply rebuke it in the name of Jesus. All power is in the name of Jesus. There is no devil or spirit that can stand against the name of Jesus. Never hesitate to use that Holy name.

A demon wants to destroy you, a beast wants to attack and ravage you, but a familiar spirit just wants to weaken you. Even when we discuss spiritual warfare and the danger of dealing with evil spirits, there is a principle similar in nature.

Consider a dead tree. It died because there was a battle going on under the surface. There was a battle that took place underneath, where nobody could see or know. When this battle took place, the goal was to weaken the tree and the host was living in the roots. In the same way, there are spirits and things that want to live beneath the surface in our lives. Frankly, I'm not worried about the things we *can* see, as much as I am about the things we *cannot* see.

You have to look at your productivity in the Kingdom and check your roots to make sure nothing has attached itself to you. Make sure that you haven't fallen in love with something that's drawing you away from God. An enemy of this type wants to steal. It wants to live and thrive off of you until there's nothing left.

In the earthly ministry of Jesus, He often talked about trees and plants. He said in Matthew 13:24-25 *"Here is another story Jesus told: 'The Kingdom of Heaven is like a farmer who planted good seed in his field. But that night as the workers slept, his enemy came and planted weeds among the wheat, then slipped away."*

This is very important. There was activity going on *at night.* Then Jesus said in Matthew 13:26-28 (NLT), *"When the crop began to grow and produce grain, the weeds also grew. The farmer's workers went to him and said, 'Sir, the field where you planted that good seed is full of weeds. Where did they come from?' 'An enemy has done this.' The farmer exclaimed."*

Can you imagine being in this story? All of a sudden, you walk out of your home and into your field, and you see weeds. Where did the weeds come from? Nobody planted them. I can relate to this story personally. I have weeds all over my yard and I haven't planted one of them. Weeds have evolved to be a powerful enemy. They have learned to survive and even thrive where they are not wanted. I am convinced that weeds take pleasure in destroying well-manicured lawns everywhere.

There are animals that specialize in living among the roots of trees. This type of animal is an unwanted host. It is an intruder and a danger to the life of the tree. This is a powerful analogy for the Kingdom of God. The enemy wants to attach itself to you at the roots to weaken and break you down to steal from you.

If you are struggling to live for God, and you can't understand why you cannot get the victory, there could be unhealthy attachments in your life. An enemy has done this. It's time to look at all aspects of your life and be prepared to adjust what you're doing. Get the enemy out of your roots before it's too late.

CONTAMINATED PEOPLE

We read in Exodus 32:7, *"And the Lord said unto Moses, Go, get thee down; …"* God said Moses you are too high. Get back down to where everybody else is. *"…for thy people, which thou broughtest out of the land of Egypt…"* Sometimes God gets upset and says, *"They're your people that you brought out,"* because they're not resembling His people. He says, *"They have corrupted themselves."*

Let's look at another danger to the health of trees. It's called *root rot*. I've never been more convinced that God was thinking about us when He made trees. If you've read the preceding chapters, you understand how much we have in common symbolically with trees. Just as trees are susceptible to dangers, *we* too are susceptible to dangers.

Trees could be affected by root rot. When we examine the definition of root rot, we discover that it causes the essential roots of the tree to decay. The roots begin to decay, and it endangers the tree's life. Some of the main causes of root rot, but not limited to these, are bad or moldy water, contaminated soil, and parasites that prey on a tree's roots. These are all dangers to the tree. Those who have to treat the tree, when they locate root rot, know that they have to first relocate the tree. They have to pull the tree out of its location in hopes of saving its life. They take the tree out of the bad situation and place it in a better environment. Sometimes God has to take us out of a bad situation and put us in a more healthy one.

Another technique to help the tree is to cut out the bad roots, sever them from the tree, in hopes of saving the good roots. All of this is in the effort of protecting the tree against root rot. Putting all this together, the Holy Ghost told me, "I want you to look up root rot, and I want you to apply it to my people because what the tree deals with physically, God's people can deal with spiritually." God said, "Protect yourself against root rot," because you may be contaminated and not know it. God wants us to shake the soil off and inspect our roots today.

You can contaminate your roots by what you allow yourself to be exposed to. When Moses leads God's people out of Egypt and they finally arrive at the mountain of God. Moses climbs the mountain to receive the plan for the future of God's people.

While he's up there, the people of God are gathered at the foot of the mountain awaiting his historic arrival with plans for their future. However, without the man of God in their midst, quickly other voices began to speak. They began to listen to contaminated people. There are some people you just don't need to listen to. God is saying, "Remove contaminated people out of your life." Get them out of your personal business. Get them out of your house. Hang up the phone. Let the phone call go to voicemail. They are contaminated and they are contagious.

These contaminated, contagious, people began causing chaos in the camp. They began to speak negatively about Moses. They began to sow seeds of discord among the camp. They began to cause division among the people of God and the more the contaminated people spoke, the more the people were infected. In the book of Exodus 32:1, *"And when the people saw that Moses delayed to come down out of the mount, the people gathered themselves unto Aaron, and said unto him, Up, make us gods, which shall go before us; for as for this Moses, the man that brought us up out of the land of Egypt, we wot not what is become of him."*

This passage of scripture takes a shocking turn when we learn that Aaron listened to the contaminated, contagious people that were talking with him. In Exodus 32:4, *"And he (Aaron) received them at their hand, and fashioned it with a graving tool, after he had made it a molten calf: and they said, these be thy gods, O Israel, which brought thee up out of the land of Egypt."*

How you can turn from the miraculous delivering power of God to building golden calves is beyond me. When you get around infected, dangerous, contaminated people, you could eventually fall into the same tragedy as the children of God did in this passage of scripture. We have to remove the contaminated people out of our lives so we can have a safe environment.

There are all kinds of sins. I know we like to focus on the physicality of sin, like murder, for example. However, it's very rare that the devil will convince a child of God to commit murder. He has to be more subtle than that. He is more prone to contaminate you. It is important that we make it a habit in our walk with God to take responsibility for our own actions. The Lord said, "they contaminated *themselves.*" There were people who talked them into it, but they were still guilty. Sin will rot your roots. You have to clip the contaminated sin out of your life. You must stop sinning. We have the power to make today the last day that we fall into sin. We can cut out the contaminated roots in our lives, whether it's a sin or a negative gossiping individual. Let's make today the last day that we entertain root rot.

Proverbs 24:16 KJV

James 4:7 KJV

1 Corinthians 15:32 KJV

Matthew 13:24-25 NLT

Matthew 13:26-28 NLT

Exodus 32:7 KJV

Exodus 32:21 KJV

Exodus 32:4 KJV

SEVEN

Look at Their Fruits

We have to understand from dealing from the topic of root rot that sin is like a severing process. We have to remove it. There is another example that I want to deal with—it's called *contamination.* Contamination doesn't get treated by cutting out roots. It gets treated by removing the tree away from the toxic source. You have to relocate it.

Gossip is talked about in scripture as a diabolical thing. Who would have thought the tongue could be so dangerous? The Bible talks about the danger of being a busybody. In other words, minding other folks' business.

There's something spiritual about how we handle one another. The Bible tells us in Galatians 6:1-2, *"Brethren, if a man be overtaken in a fault, ye which are spiritual, restore such an one in the spirit of meekness; considering thyself, lest thou also be tempted. Bear ye one another's burdens, and so fulfill the law of Christ."* God puts the title *spiritual* on people who restore those who have fallen. I wonder what title God gives people who talk about people that have fallen?

When somebody comes to you and they're bringing negativity, you have to understand that by bringing that negativity, it ought to tell you something about them. When someone comes with that kind of spirit, it also comes with an atmosphere. The atmosphere for us is like soil to the tree. We feed on the spiritual atmosphere around us. We know when something doesn't feel right.

Isn't it interesting that when somebody brings up a certain subject the atmosphere will radiate that subject? Have you ever been in a setting, and the conversation turns negative? Isn't it interesting that the atmosphere mirrors our conversations? Something always comes in, and something always goes out based on the conversations you keep.

That's why it says in James 3:10 (NLT), *"And so blessing and cursing come pouring out of the same mouth. Surely, my brothers and sisters, this is not right."* James brings out an important revelation. We need to guard our tongues and take seriously the words we speak. The child of God should not cuss. Cursing is the opposite of blessing. Blessing creates an atmosphere of peace and salvation. However, cursing creates the opposite atmosphere of negativity and condemnation. Demons operate in negative environments. The things of God are nurtured in Holy environments.

SOUL WINNING

Why does a tree go through all of this effort to make fruit? The tree is enticing animals to eat its fruit because of the seed. The tree needs the seed to be planted someplace else. This ensures the creation of more trees. This is a great analogy of soul winning. If you get involved in the work of God, you will help ensure the growth of the kingdom of God. When we win souls, we are simply spreading the seed of the gospel of Jesus Christ. Someone told me something many years ago that God blesses soul winners and He'll do anything for a soul winner.

So, in my conclusion, let me encourage you all to be like the tree that is planted by the rivers of water. Make sure you follow the encouragement in this book so that you can go and bring forth fruit and you will have a great and eternal reward in glory.

Galatians 6:1-2 KJV
James 3:10 NLT

Made in the USA
Monee, IL
15 November 2024

70215603R00056